CINZIA RANDAZZO

The Concept of the Education of the Young People at the First Origins of the Christianity:
Features of Educational Approach for the Lay ones

Youcanprint *Self-Publishing*

Title | The Concept of the Education of the Young People at the First Origins of the Christianity: Features of Educational Approach for the Lay ones
Author | Cinzia Randazzo
ISBN | 978-88-93219-09-9

Printed on November 2015

Youcanprint Self-Publishing
Corso Roma, 73 - 73039 Tricase (LE) - Italy

www.youcanprint.it
info@youcanprint.it
Facebook: facebook.com/youcanprint.it
Twitter: twitter.com/youcanprintit

INDEX

PREFACE

Cinzia Randazzo has kindly provided me with a draft English translation of her Italian essay "The Education of Young People and the Origins of Christianity." This is an important topic, and one that has not, Randazzo asserts, been adequately addressed by scholars of early Christianity. Here, she examines the literature of the subapostolic period, particularly the writings of Clement of Rome, the *Shepherd of Hermas*, Polycarp and the *Didachē*. Her aims are not simply historical and literary, but theological and pedagogical, seeking for guidance from the early Christian writers regarding the education and Christian formation of children and youth in the present.

There is a great deal to admire in the writings of these ancient Christian educators. These are men who were passionately concerned about the future of the church, and were acutely aware of the importance of youth in the transmission and defence of their faith. Many of their ideas are instructive for Christian education today: the insight that teaching is a dialectical process that requires engagement on the part of both the teacher and the pupil; the importance of the teacher as role model; the need for Christ-like humility on the part of the educator; the virtue of wisdom. Other aspects of their teaching, which reflect the philosophy and educational theory of their time, may be less appealing: the spirit-flesh dichotomy, the emphasis on discipline and punishment, the harsh judgements envisioned for those who stray from the righteous path.

This is a preliminary study, and thus it raises additional questions in the mind of the reader. Although Randazzo briefly discusses the role of women in the education of children, the question of women as teachers (1 Tim 2:12; cf. Acts 18:26; Polycarp, *Letter to the Philippians* 4:2) begs for further attention, since, as Margaret Y. MacDonald has argued, the domestic space of the earliest churches no doubt functioned as home schools for children and adults alike.[1] Did Christian children continue to study in schools run by pagan schoolmasters, or did their communities attempt to provide a distinctively Christian curriculum to replace (or supplement) Graeco-Roman *paideia*? Did girls receive the same quality of religious instruction as the boys, and if not, how does this square with the famous

---

[1] Margaret Y. MacDonald, *The Power of Children: The Construction of Families in the Greco-Roman World* (Waco, TX: Baylor University Press, 2014), 109-48.

baptismal formula of Galatians 3:28? Where did slave members of the ecclesia fit into Christian *paideia*, as students and as teachers? Did free members of the church balk at being instructed by slaves, as some early Christian men resisted instruction by women? I hope that these, and other questions raised in this study, will be investigated in Cinzia Randazzo's future publications.

Saskatoon (Canada) 21-9-2015

Mary Ann Beavis, Ph.D.
Professor
Department of Religion and Culture
St. Thomas More College
The University of Saskatchewan

This latest work of the author, who has already published several works about the apostolic fathers, aims at offering us a survey of the ideas about education of the earliest Christian writers from the end of the first century to the middle of the second. Her contribution is divided into two main sections. In the first one she looks over the role of the parents and the other adults of the Christian community in this process. First she emphasizes that in the mind of the earliest Christian writers, *e.g.* Clement, one of the earliest bishops of Rome, education is a dialectic process: educators are not above its progression, but they are integral part of it. Those responsible must be very much involved in this duty. What they constantly have to keep in mind is God's justice. Being alert at all times, they can effectively counteract the bad influences of the evil spirits, who love corruptible things and are also fond of lying.

After describing the process of education and the menaces threatening young people, our author treats the main virtues which are in the focus of Christian education. Especially two early Christian works serve didactic purposes: the *Didache* (popular particularly in the Christian East) and the *Pastor* attributed to the Hermas, a layman living in Italy. The dangers of the rebellion of young people and the great responsibility of the adults are especially emphasized by Clement of Rome and the *Didache*.

Through education young people should get in possession of the following virtues: moderation in everything, appreciation of human dignity, temperance, and they also have to learn how to fear God. Clement enumerates several biblical examples and he emphasizes also the responsibility of the whole Christian community. His ideas harmonize with the pieces of advice given by the so-called *Letter to Diognetus* and those of Saint Polycarp.

We have to observe that unlike in pagan society, women are not excluded from the education of the Christian youth. On the contrary, they have the responsibility of bringing up their children so that they may be able to lead a pious life.

In the second main section the author describes the models for Christian education: Christ himself and Christian wise men. Christ set an example for us especially by his humility, fulfilling Isaiah's prophecy: being obedient to his Father's will, he tolerated suffering even on the cross for our salvation. But also during the whole course of his life he preserved his purity from the contamination of sins, as all Christian people should, emphasizes Polycarp.

However, not only Christ should be our role model in our Christian life, but – as Clement reminds us – his faithful followers, some of them rich in experience and wisdom, who are showing the right path to our salvation. The anonymous author of the *Martyrdom of Polycarp* introduces us also a young person, a certain Germanicus, who had been trained in Christian *paideia*, *i.e.* education. He becomes a model of a Christian educator, who strengthens his fellow martyrs in their suffering to bear witness to Christ.

This survey about early Christian moral education widens our horizon in this field of patristic research to a considerable extent. Other scholars (*e.g.* V. Monachino and A. Turck) concentrated mainly on the *curricula*, the didactic material presented by the earliest catechists, while Dr Randazzo offers us also a summary of the moral content of early Christian *paideia*.

Budapest 12-10-2015

László Perendy
Pázmány Péter Catholic University,
Budapest

INTRODUCTION

Purpose of this research is to study the concept of education and not of catechesis in the works of the Apostolic Fathers because, as far as we know it, a punctual and in depth study on such texts has not yet been undertaken, ever since the researchers have mostly examined the subject matter in the texts that go back to the apologetic[2] and late-ancient

---

[2] T. GEORGES, *Justin's School at Rome: Reflections on Early Christian "Schools"*, in P. GEMEINHARDT, T. GEORGES, (éds.), *Between Education and Conversion. Ways of Approaching Religion in Late Antiquity*, Berlin/Boston 2012 =*Zeitschrift für antikes Christentum* 16,1, pp. 75-87; P. GEMEINHARDT, *In Search of Christian Paideia Education and Conversion in Early Christian Biography* , in P. GEMEINHARDT, T. GEORGES, (éds.), *Between Education and Conversion. Ways of Approaching Religion in Late Antiquity*, Berlin/Boston 2012 =*Zeitschrift für antikes Christentum* 16,1, pp. 88-98. For a general panoramic on the theme of the education in the ancient Christianity see H.I. MARROU, *Histoire de l'éducation dans l'antiquité*, Éditions du Seuil 1965; M.M. MITCHELL-F.M. YOUNG, *The Cambridge History of Christianity*, vol. 1,

period,[3] by not excluding that medieval and contemporary.[4]

From such works it is deduced that the argument is divided in two lines which are the

---

Origins to Constantine, Cambridge University Press 2008, pp. 82-487.

[3] See H. von SCHUBERT (trad. it. di G. SANNA), *Istruzione ed educazione alle origini del cristianesimo*, Venezia 1929; E. KEVANE, *Translatio Imperii: Augustine's De doctrina christiana and the classical paideia*, in *Studia patristica*, vol 14 (1976), pp. 446-460; St. SHOEMAKER, *Gnosis and Paideia: Education and Heresy in Late Ancient Egypt*, in *Studia Patristica* vol. 31 (1997), pp. 535-539; A. HILARION, *O Theological Education in the Christian East: first to sixt centuries* in J. BEHR-A. LOUTH-D. CONOMOS (Eds), *Abba. The tradition of Orthodoxy in the West. Festschrift for Bishop Kallistos (Ware) of Diokleia*, Crestwood, NY. ST Vladimir's Seminary Press 2003, pp. 43-64; B. SURIEL, *Christian Education and the Fathers of the Church in Alexandria in Late Antiquity*, in *Studia Patristica* 39 (2006), pp. 441-446; R. CRIBIORE, *Higher education in early Byzantine Egypt: rhetoric, Latin and the Law*, in R.S. BAGNAL (Ed.), *Egypt in the Byzantine World 300-700*, Cambridge 2007, pp. 47-66; N.A. HENEIN, *Le monachisme egyptien révélateur de l'âme copte*, Limoges 2008, pp. 322-326; P. GEMEINHARDT, *Holiness and Education in Late Antique Hagiography*, in *Studia Patristica* 44 (2010), pp. 521-526; B.

special object of study in this work: the first

pertinent to the educational role of the parents

and of the adults and the other pertinent to the

educational model for the young people. In the

____

LEYERLE, *Children and 'the Child' in Early Christianity*, in J.E. GRUBBS-T. PARKIN (Eds.), *The Oxford Handbook of Childhood and Education in the Classical World,*, Oxford University Press 2013, pp. 559-579; S. RUBENSON, *The Formation and Reformations of the Sayings of the Desert Fathers*, in *Studia Patristica* 55,3 (2013), 5-22; S. RUBENSON, *Transformative Light and Luminous Tradition in Early Christian Mysticism and Monasticism*, in *Svensk Teologisk Kvartalskrift* 90.4 (2014), pp. 179-187; A.B. HUIZENGA, *Clement's Use of Female Role Models as a Pedagogical Strategy*, Oxford 2015 in press; M. QUIRCIO, *Religious Education and the Health of the Soul according to Basil of Caesarea and the Emperor Julian*, Oxford 2015, in press; S. GEORGIEVA, *The Letters of Jerome, Augustine and Pelagius to the Virgin Demetrias. The Epistolary Education of Early Christianity*, in *Studia Patristica* 74 (2016), pp. 329-340; D. RIGHI (a cura di), *Educazione, paideia cristiana e immagini di Chiesa*. Atti del convegno della Facoltà teologica dell'Emilia Romagna, Bologna, 29-30 novembre 2011, EDB, Bologna 2016; J. STRAWBRIDGE, *'A School of Paul? Pauline Texts in Early Christian Schooltext Papyri.'* in M. HAUGE-A. PITTS (Eds), *Ancient Education and Early Christianity* (LNTS; New York: T&T Clark 2016); J.I.O. van't

first line the Fathers attribute to the educational role of the adults a virtual meaning, that is the special object of study in this contribution: their education towards the young people is aimed at edifying the young people to the virtues of the justice, of the moderation, of the dignity, of the God's fear and of the temperance. In the second line the apostolic Fathers attribute to the educational model of the young people that of Christ and that of the true Christian wise men, making

WESTEINDE, *Teach and Transform: Education and Reconstructing Identity in Jerome's Letters*, in *Studia Patristica* 74 (2016), pp. 223-238.

[4] D. WERNER – D. ESTERLINE- N. KANG – J. RAJA (Eds), *REGNUM STUDIES IN GLOBAL CHRISTIANITY, Handbook of Theological Education in World Christianity, Theological Perspective – Regional Surveys – Ecumenical Trends*, Oxford 2010; A. BRENT, *Philosophy and Educational Foundations*, Routledge Library Editions 2016; D. RIGHI (a cura di), *Educazione, paideia cristiana e immagini di Chiesa.* Atti del convegno della Facoltà teologica dell'Emilia Romagna, Bologna, 29-30 novembre 2011, EDB, Bologna 2016.

reference, to testimony of the second model, to the figure of Germanic.

Inside such lines it is articulated the present work. With regard to first line it is sought to not only individuate the conditions that allow the educational activity and the education to the above-mentioned virtues, but also the effects that spring from these. Concerning the second line it is sought to highlight the *virtual* fundamentals on which the educational model of Christ not only is based, but also that of the faithful and wise men, included Germanic.

A return to the apostolic Fathers is therefore opportune for the today's educators, because it is not possible to try to educate the young people without knowing the thought of such Fathers, since it is from there that it is born the new Christian education, founded upon the God's fear.

1. THE EDUCATIONAL ROLE OF THE PARENTS AND OF THE ADULTS

1.1. *The Concept of Education*

1.1.1. Circular Condition

Fundamental condition, without which the education of the young people is not possible, is the presence of the little ones: "*The adults cannot stay without the little ones and the little ones without the adults*".[5] Clement of Rome shows that the adult cannot impart the education to the little ones if these ones are not there and vice versa. The activity of the educating is possible because of the presence of the educator (wise adult) and of the one who is to be educated (little young, child), because if there is not one of the two, such exercising is null.

Such activity is not only reversible because it can lose its effectiveness when one of the two parts is missing but also circular, since the education is based on the communication between the two interlocutors (educator and one who is to be educated). In this communication it emerges the connection

---

[5] CLEMENT of Rome, *Epistle to the Corinthians* 37,4. Ed. crit. F.X. FUNK-K. BIHLMEYER-M. WHITTAKER, *Die Apostolischen Väter. Griechisch-deutsche Parallelausgabe*, p. 120. Trad. di A. QUACQUARELLI, *I Padri Apostolici*, p. 74.

between the two subjects: "*in all the things there is some connection and in this the utility*".[6] Because there is the education the educating one, according to Clement, has the obligation to instaurate a communicative circularity with the one who is on the point of being educated because between the two there is connection and dialogic interaction. The image that Clement uses to point out this, is that of the body and of his members:

> The head cannot be without the feet, neither the feet without the head. The smallest parts of our body are necessary and usefuls to the whole body; but all the parts cohabit and have an only subordination to save the whole body.[7]

This educational circularity between the emitting one (educator) and the receptor (the one who is to be educated) is appanage of that educational circularity that is instaurated between Father and Son in *protological* Saturday yet before the creation; both circularities are aimed at the salvation: the first because is at the base of the salvation of the one

---

[6] *Ibidem*

[7] CLEMENT of Rome, *Epistle to the Corinthians* 37,5. Ed. crit. F.X. FUNK-K. BIHLMEYER-M. WHITTAKER, *Die Apostolischen Väter. Griechisch-deutsche Parallelausgabe*, p. 120. Trad. di A. QUACQUARELLI, *I Padri Apostolici*, p. 74.

who is to be educated, since the one who is educated is formed to desire only the Good in all the things, so that in this walk of progressive similarity to God, he saves himself, the second because is cause of the creation, that is to say of the removal of the darkness and of the manifesting itself of the light,

1.1.2. Virtual Conditions

Because one become good educator it is necessary to flee the way of the death, avoiding to make the following acts:
– to persecute the good ones:
Persecutor (διῶκται) of the good persons (.). By them is distant the calm and the patience; they are lovers of the vain things, (.) killers of the children.[8]
The persecutors are wrapped from a spirit of torment, whose litmus test is reflected in that group of demons that impute to Christ the cause of their torment, while instead are theirs the bearers of such discomfort, because their spirit is not turned towards the supernal things (Mt 8,28-29).

---

[8] *Didachè* 5,2. Ed. crit. F.X. FUNK-K. BIHLMEYER-M. WHITTAKER, *Die Apostolischen Väter. Griechisch-deutsche Parallelausgabe*, p. 10. Trad. di A. QUACQUARELLI, *I Padri Apostolici*, p. 33.

These spirits are already in prey to the torment, because directs to satisfy their negative impulses opposites to those tense to the search of the Truth. From such framework the persecutors are the ones who are strongly attracted by this horrible carnal thirst of molestation and of torment because their soul is not in peace with God, since it is away from Him, why these ones are denominated *"children's killers."* The true educator is instead the one who is mild and serene as Christ, who doesn't let himself torment, because his spirit is permanently in tuning with that of the Father:

> You take my yoke above you and
> learn from me, that I'm mild and
> humble of heart, and you will find
> comfort for your souls (Mt 11,29).

- To hate the truth. For the author of the *Didachè* it is not a good educator the one who hates the Truth: *"Haters of the Truth* (.) *children's killers".*[9]

The one who hates the Truth follows the negative tendencies of the flesh that make him slave of his own carnal instincts and subdued to their desires. On the contrary the denial of themselves is the main way to follow the Truth:

> Who loves the father or the mother

---

[9] *Ibidem*

more than me is not worthy of me;
who loves the son or the daughter
more than me is not worthy of me
(Mt 10,37).
– To love the lie: *"lovers of the lie* (.)
children's killers".[10] The ones who follow
the lie are compared to Adam and Eve
who followed the word of the snake that
before deceived Eve and then Adam (Gen
2-3).
– To ignore the prize of the justice:
"unawares of the prize of the justice".[11]

The author of the *Didachè* retakes the
pauline thought, why every Christian has the
task of running to reach the prize of the justice,
on the model of the athletes who are intents to
run for receiving the final prize in the stadium
(1Cor 9,24-25).
The true educators of the faith have the task of
always having the stare at the God's justice, to
prepare oneself to educate the children with
perseverance in the faith in Christ.
– Do not adhere to the good and to the
righteous judgment: *"do not adhering to
the good or to the righteous*

---

[10] *Ibidem*

[11] *Ibidem*

judgment".[12] For the author of the *Didachè* the Christians are called to seek the Good and to judge rightly. On behalf of the Christian it is needed a period of preparation and of constancy in the faith, on the trail of the first letter of Paul to the Cor 9,27. The progressive walk of the Christian is not turned to the return, that is to say in the condition where he left, but to a superior goal, so that he become similar to the Father.

– To keep under control the evil. Every Christian educator knows that during the walk there is the obligation to be vigilant for doing not falling in temptation, in line with what Jesus told his disciples (Mt 26,40-41). The motives that are at the base of such deviant attitudes are the followings:
– the love for the corruptible things
– the lack of the calm and of the patience
– the lack of the God's fear, since there is not the feeling of the gratitude towards God who has created them:
From them it is distant the calm and the patience; they are lovers of the vain

---

[12] *Ibidem*

things, avids of the reward, merciless
with the poor men, intolerants with who
is oppressed, not gratefuls towards whom
created them; children's killers, destroyers
of the God's creature, careless of the
needy.[13]

1.2. *Education to the Justice*

1.2.1. Conditions

The lack of anger, for the *Shepherd*
of Hermas, is another condition because the
child is educated:
You Hermas do not be angry with your
children or to neglect your sister because
they are purified from their sins before.
They will be educated with a just address
if you won't bear them resentment. The
resentment produces the death.[14]

The lack of the resentment, that is to say
of the grudge or of the continuous hate, allows
the parent to educate the child according to

---

[13] *Ibidem*

[14] HERMAS, *Shepherd. Vision* 2,7,1. Ed. crit. F.X. FUNK-K.
BIHLMEYER-M. WHITTAKER, *Die Apostolischen Väter.
Griechisch-deutsche Parallelausgabe*, p. 340. Trad. di A.
QUACQUARELLI, *I Padri Apostolici*, p. 248.

"*justice.*"[15] Here Hermas refers to the justice of Christ, intending with this do not give to the child what is due to him, but to educate the him following the optic of the conversion of the heart in function of the purification of his sins, because it is instaurated between parents and children a educational circularity based on the love (pardon) and not on the grudge.

To the child it is imparted a education based on the reconciliation with God who makes lever or it has its pivot on the justice, that is to say on the conversion of the heart that allows the pardon and the purification of the sins.

1.2.2. Effects

According to the author of the *Didachè* are reputed "*the children's killers*" the parents who follow the way of the death:

> The way of the death is this. First
> of all it is bad and full of curse:
> homicides (.) 2. Persecutor of the

---

[15] HERMAS, *Shepherd. Vision* 2,7,1.3.4. Ed. crit. F.X. FUNK-K. BIHLMEYER-M. WHITTAKER, *Die Apostolischen Väter. Griechisch-deutsche Parallelausgabe*, p. 340. Trad. di A. QUACQUARELLI, *I Padri Apostolici*, pp. 248-249.

good ones (.) the children's killers.[16]

The parent who kills the child is sower of death because he does not consider the child to be a creature of God: "*Destroyers of the creature of God*".[17] The author of the *Didachè* explains that the killers of the children are that circle of parents who consider the child a object and subdued to their will. This way of behaving injures, in line with the God's commandment "*do not kill*" (Deut 5,17), the dignity of the child, of the same parents and of the same God who has created them both. In line with the "*principle*" of Gen 1, all the living beings are creatures of God, because moulded by the hands of the same God who has blown in the nostrils the vital breath, that is a particle of his spirit.

From this framework the parents are not kept to consider the children "*his ownership*", but "*God's ownership*" as themselves, since all the living beings are children of the same God who has created them. Another form of moral

---

[16] *Didachè* 5,1.2. Ed. crit. F.X. FUNK-K. BIHLMEYER-M. WHITTAKER, *Die Apostolischen Väter. Griechisch-deutsche Parallelausgabe*, p. 10. Trad. di A. QUACQUARELLI, *I Padri Apostolici*, pp. 32-33.

[17] *Didachè* 5,2. Ed. crit. F.X. FUNK-K. BIHLMEYER-M. WHITTAKER, *Die Apostolischen Väter. Griechisch-deutsche Parallelausgabe*, p. 10. Trad. di A. QUACQUARELLI, *I Padri Apostolici*, p. 33.

deviance is the rebellion of the young people against the old people: "*So rebelled themselves (.) the young ones against the old ones*".[18] According to Clement of Rome such form of rebellion is caused by the fact that the young people abandoned the fear of God, since don't behave according to the commandments of the Lord, because they follow the passions of their wicked heart:

> For this are gone away the justice and the peace, since each one has abandoned the fear of God and has darkened his faith; he does not walk according to the divine commandments, doesn't behave as it is worthwhile for Christ, but he proceeds according to the passions of his wicked heart.[19]

The rebellion of the young people is imputable, according to Clement of Rome, to the progressive going away of the young people from the God's fear, that is to say from the lack of giving to God respect, reverence and

---

[18] CLEMENT of Rome, *Epistle to the Corinthians* 3,3. Ed. crit. F.X. FUNK-K. BIHLMEYER-M. WHITTAKER, *Die Apostolischen Väter. Griechisch-deutsche Parallelausgabe*, p. 82. Trad. di A. QUACQUARELLI, *I Padri Apostolici*, p. 51.

[19] CLEMENT of Rome, *Epistle to the Corinthians* 3,4. Ed. crit. F.X. FUNK-K. BIHLMEYER-M. WHITTAKER, *Die Apostolischen Väter. Griechisch-deutsche Parallelausgabe*, pp. 82-84. Trad. di A. QUACQUARELLI, *I Padri Apostolici*, p. 51.

attention as to a friend.

This form of overcoming, that is manifested in the rebellion of the young people against all what God has created, - included the old ones – is daughter of the jealousy, which is cause, for Clement, of the eternal death.[20] In Clement it recurs the thought of Sap 2,24 that it will be retaken in Rm 5,12:

> Then, as because of an only man the sin has entered in the world and with the sin the death, so also the death has reached all the men, because all have sinned.

Returning to the author of the *Didachè*, he exhorts the adults to abstain from corrupting the boys: *"Do not contaminate (παιδοφθορήσεις) the boys"*.[21] The verb παιδοφθορεῖν, coming from παῖς (boy) + φθείρω (to ruin),[22] is employed by the author of the *Didaché* to show that the adults have the task of doing not corrupting the boys, that is do not make to turn their desires entirely towards the things of the earth that are corruptible. It

---

[20] *Ibidem*

[21] *Didaché* 2,2. Ed. crit. F.X. FUNK-K. BIHLMEYER-M. WHITTAKER, *Die Apostolischen Väter. Griechisch-deutsche Parallelausgabe*, Tübingen 1992, p. 6. Trad. di A. QUACQUARELLI, *I Padri Apostolici*, Roma 2000, p. 30.

[22] T. HOLTZ, *Φθείρω*, in H. BALZ-G. SCHNEIDER, *Dizionario esegetico del Nuovo Testamento*, vol. II, Brescia 1998, col. 1788-1792.

emerges the pauline sense of the corruption of the terrestrial life, because all what belongs to the terrestrial life is imprinted to the transient, to the temporary (1 Cor 9,25) and aimed at the consumption of the things, to their destruction (Col 2,22) and not to the eternal values. The author of the *Didachè*, in line with the Pauline thought, expresses the intention to avoid that the boys count limitedly on their creatural character, because their present reality is turned to the dissolution, to the death that is proper of this world. It resounds the pauline antithesis between terrestrial corruptibility and celestial incorruptibility (Rm 2,7); for this motive every adult is kept to orientate the boys towards the gifts of the Spirit because these are incorruptible, so that, drinking to such gifts, they can become incorruptible, enjoying already on the earth the true eternal fruits of the Spirit.

1.3. *Education to the Moderation and to the Dignity*

Clement of Rome turns to the Corinthians his gratifying appeal to have been faithful to the law of the Lord, since they have also instilled in the young people the sense of the moderation and of the dignity:

> You exhorted the young people to
> think (νοεῖν) moderate (μέτρια) and
> worthy (σεμνὰ) things ".[23]

The persons responsible of the community of Corinth are undertaken to turn the mind of the young ones towards the just equilibrium with the purpose to orientate their thought towards the things that don't exceed or don't decrease the just measure of all the things. Concrete has been their will to make moderate the mind of the young people, so that they know to measure all the things with just measure and to give to every thing the just due, that is to say what is due to them without excesses and neither regresses. They have implemented in the mind of the young people the virtue of the moderation, through which they tend to give to every thing what is due.

Besides to orientate the mind of the young people towards the virtue of the moderation the persons responsible are undertaken to haul the thought of the young people towards worthy things that God likes, that don't offend the modesty and that don't

---

[23] CLEMENT of Rome, *Epistle to the Corinthians* 1,3. Ed. crit. F.X. FUNK-K. BIHLMEYER-M. WHITTAKER, *Die Apostolischen Väter. Griechisch-deutsche Parallelausgabe*, p. 80. Trad. di A. QUACQUARELLI, *I Padri Apostolici*, p. 50.

injure the sense of the good course of the civil living; sense springing from the image of God who is placed in every man. The persons responsible of the community are direct to give to the young people theoretical examples imprinted to the dignity; examples that have the finality to turn the thought of the young people towards things that build the humanity according to the salvific project of God, going away them so from all the unhealthies thoughts that drag them towards unbridled and disordered impulses that inevitably conduct them towards the perdition, the disgregation of their psico-physical being and not towards the unity of their same being. It recurs in the *Epistle to the Corinthians* the exhortatory accent, turned to the young people, of the *Epistle to Titus*. In 2,6 Paul is turned to Titus because he exhorts the young people to "*to be judicious*" (Tt 2,6): "*It still exhorts the more young people to be judicious (σωφρονεῖν)* " (Tt 2,6). In the *Epistle to Titus* such oral expression is index of moderation[24]; virtue that is lived by those who choose to live an intense rational life, "*that consists in the refusal of worldly*

---

[24] See D. ZELLER, *σώφρων*, in H. BALZ – G. SCHNEIDER, *Dizionario Esegetico del Nuovo Testamento*, vol. 2, col. 1558.

desires."[25] To the adults it's up the obligation to make the young people judicious, giving them a adequate psico-physics and virtual formation that makes them worthy of being simple and reserved, so that their reserve be appanage of the dignity of God who has created the man simple and moderate, because he be not pompous and affected in his thoughts. The young ones are not exhorted to pompously exalt their qualities to the detriment of the others, but to become, in front of the others, living mirror of the reserved and judicious simplicity of God, where the word is not empty and direct to itself as in the charlatan, but it is united to the action, why the two things are not untied but united, on the model of God who speaks little and fulfils great things: "*God said: «Be the light», and the light was*" (Gen 1,1).

1.4. *Education to the God's Fear*

Clement of Rome exhorts the Corinthians to educate the young people to the God's fear: "*We educate (παιδεύωμεν) the young people to the God's fear (φόβου)*".[26]

---

[25] *Ibidem*

[26] CLEMENT of Rome, *Epistle to the Corinthians* 21,6. Ed. crit. F.X. FUNK-K. BIHLMEYER-M. WHITTAKER, *Die Apostolischen Väter. Griechisch-deutsche Parallelausgabe*, p. 104. Trad. di A.

Clement of Rome, to do relive in the young people the sense of the attention and of the respect towards God, uses the verb παιδεύειν that, in the Greek antiquity, designated

the education and the care of the little boy who growing will enter to take part in the world of the adults and he therefore needs of guide, teaching, instruction and together with a certain constraint, that is to say of the discipline and also of the punishment.[27]

Such form verbal comes from παιδεία, with which term it is indicated "*the walk that the education and the formation must go along and it is also the destination to reach*".[28] The term παιδεία implicates the experience and the admonishment as conditions for the educator, initials and essentials to guide the little boy through the teaching of his fundamental notions. At the base of all these, the educator aims "*to do hate what is detestable and to love what is lovable.*".[29] It belongs to the sphere of the Truth and of the highest Good what is

---

QUACQUARELLI, *I Padri Apostolici*, p. 64.

[27] G. BERTRAM, παιδεύω, in G. KITTEL-G. FRIEDRICH, *Grande Lessico del Nuovo Testamento*, vol. IX, col. 106.

[28] *Ibidem*

[29] PLATO, Leggi 2,653 c.

lovable, why the educator aims at cultivating the virtues of the Spirit because the young people can be educated according to his teaching.

Returning to the *Epistle to the Corinthians* to the persons responsible it's up the obligation not only to be of the good educators, from whom it shines a good behaviour of life but also of the good instructors, because they can instruct the young people in the true παιδεία, that is to say in the immortal virtues of the Spirit, putting themselves in guard, in line with the Aristotelian thought, against the vain tendencies of the flesh.[30]

From such framework the exhortation to the education (paideia) implicates for the educators, from a side, their behaviour of life that become exemplary to the young one because it is lived according to the divine model of the true education that in itself is immortal and divine[31] and, from the other, the teaching of the same, through the oral form of the admonishment. To the educator therefore it's up the task to be a person who has really God's fear, ever since the education of the young

---

[30] ARISTOTLE, *Etica nicomachea* 1336b23.

[31] See SOCRATES in PLATO, *Clit.* 407a

people is to be aimed at the God's fear.

The God's fear is one of the virtues that conducts the man to have reverence, attention and respect towards God[32], to consider him as a friend why the adults, responsible of the community of Corinth, are kept to be the more wise than the community because only these ones are called, according to the ancient socratic adage, to educate the young people to the fear of God: *"the more wise man educated to the God's fear and to the regal dignity"*.[33]

On the base of their wisdom and of their true behaviour lived according to the virtue of the God's fear, the adults of the community of Corinth were primarily designated for this task and, consequently, for teaching such virtue, undertaking, together with the young people, to make such formative walk. The young ones were educated to the God's fear that is not the simple knowledge of God, since, retaking the words of the anonymous author of the *To Diognetus*, the knowledge without the love inflates while the love for the true life edifies.[34]

---

[32] See C. RANDAZZO, *La teologia del timore di Dio agli esordi del cristianesimo*, Tricase 2014, 12-22.

[33] Ps. PLATONE, *Alcibiade* 1,121e-122a

[34] *To Diognetus* 12,5. Ed. crit. F.X. FUNK-K. BIHLMEYER-M. WHITTAKER, *Die Apostolischen Väter. Griechisch-deutsche Parallelausgabe*, p. 322. Trad. di E. NORELLI, *A Diogneto*, Milano

The simple knowledge of God without the love for him doesn't edify because the man becomes aware of knowing many things but he does not bear fruit, since doesn't love the true life.[35]

From this, it is deducted that the young ones are not only educated to know God, but to love him so as to have him always near to make him part integral of their life, without whom the man would lose the sense of the true life and his same image of man tense to desire the supernal things. In Clement it resounds the thought of the *To Diognetus* 12,6-7, because the educator has not only the task to do know to the one who is to be educated the virtue of the God's fear but to arouse in him the desire to love God, to welcome him in his heart, so that, through the knowledge, united to the virtue of the God's fear, the young one can reach the true knowledge of God and to love the true life.

Particularly Polycarp specifies that the women have the task to educate their children: *"Moreover that your women (...) educate the children in the God's fear"*.[36] The exhortation of

1991, p. 130.

[35] *To Diognetus* 12,6. Ed. crit. F.X. FUNK-K. BIHLMEYER-M. WHITTAKER, *Die Apostolischen Väter. Griechisch-deutsche Parallelausgabe*, p. 322. Trad. di E. NORELLI, *A Diogneto*, Milano 1991, p. 130.

[36] POLYCARP, *Letter to the philippians* 4,2. Ed. crit. F.X. FUNK-K.

Polycarp is turned to the women who have the duty to educate the children, showing so that the woman has integral part as the man in the education of the children. It is thus rediscovered the feminine role in the education of the children; role that in the Jewish tradition and in the pauline thought was attributed only to the father.[37]

The woman assumes for Polycarp an active role in the education of the children to the God's fear, on condition that

> they walk in the faith given to them, in the charity, in the purity and having a preference for their husbands in every fidelity and loving equally all the people in the chastity.[38]

Other condition, because the parent can instaurate a correct and educational circularity with the child, is the teaching of the God's fear:

Do not send away the hand from

BIHLMEYER-M. WHITTAKER, *Die Apostolischen Väter. Griechisch-deutsche Parallelausgabe*, p. 248. Trad. di A. QUACQUARELLI, *I Padri Apostolici*, p. 155.

[37] G. BERTRAM, παιδεύω, in G. KITTEL-G. FRIEDRICH, *Grande Lessico del Nuovo Testamento*, vol. IX, col. 129. Vedi anche Ef 6,4.

[38] POLYCARP, *Letter to the philippians* 4,2. Ed. crit. F.X. FUNK-K. BIHLMEYER-M. WHITTAKER, *Die Apostolischen Väter. Griechisch-deutsche Parallelausgabe*, 248. Trad. di A. QUACQUARELLI, *I Padri Apostolici*, p. 155.

your child and from your daughter,
but from the infancy you will teach
them the God's fear (φόβον).[39]

At the base of the education of the child there is the instruction or better the knowledge of the God's fear on behalf of the parents. To them it's up the obligation to furnish to the child the following instructions about the virtue of the God's fear:

- The God's fear in positive sense. It is not the God's fear but the respectful moderation, or better the respect that who desires God turns towards him.

— The person who has God's fear has the obligation to have a good moderation of God, because he loves him and desires him above all the things.

— In whatever circumstance of the daily life the person who has God's fear is called to abandon oneself in the God's hands, confident of his intervention in his favor and of his salvation and protection.

— To the person who has God's fear it's up the duty to be subdued to God and to turn to him the due respect and the due

---

[39]   BARNABAS, *Epistola* 19,5. Ed. crit. F.X. FUNK-K. BIHLMEYER-M. WHITTAKER, *Die Apostolischen Väter. Griechisch-deutsche Parallelausgabe*, p. 70. Trad. di A. QUACQUARELLI, *I Padri Apostolici*, p. 212.

reverence.

1.5. *Reciprocal Education according to the Sign of the Temperance*

Other condition, according to the *Shepherd* of Hermas, - because every responsible of the community can become a good educator - is the reciprocal education, imparted according to the virtue of the temperance:

This intemperance is harmful for you who possess and doing not giving to the needy people (.) 6. You be careful that boast of your wealth, that the needy people are never afflicted and their complain doesn't ascend to the Lord. With your goods it is not closed the door of the tower 7. I tell to you who be the heads of the church and you occupy the first places: you don't do yourselves similar to the wizards. The wizards bring their filters in the little vases, you bring your filter, the poison, in the heart. 8. You be hardened and don't want to purify yourselves, to melt your feeling in the pure heart to obtain mercy by the great king (.). 10. How can you educate the men chosen by God, if you be not educated? Educate yourselves, therefore, in turn and you live in peace because I can in presence of the Father be happy to talk about you all,. [40]

The church, symbolized as an elderly woman, exhorts the heads of the church to reciprocally educate themselves to the virtue of the temperance - virtue that consists in the giving to the needy people what is due for the necessary food and sustenance – since such mutual education bears to live in the peace and not in the discord. Here the church exhorts the heads of the church to doing not multiplying their wealths and their material well-being to the detriment of the increasing poverty of the needy people, victims of the abuse and of the abandonment on behalf of the rich men. The church exhorts to the charity (love) towards the needy people; love that comes from the virtue of the temperance, according to which the man undertakes to give to the needy people what is necessary to him, with the remuneration of doing not increasing his wealths. It's up, according to Herrmas, to the heads of the

[40] HERMAS, *Shepherd,Vision* 3,17,4.6.7.8.10. Ed. crit. F.X. FUNK-K. BIHLMEYER-M. WHITTAKER, *Die Apostolischen Väter. Griechisch-deutsche Parallelausgabe*, pp. 358-360. Trad. di A. QUACQUARELLI, *I Padri Apostolici*, pp. 258-259.

church the reciprocal education to such virtue, ever since that they excel in goods and possessions of material nature.

The virtue of the intemperance, to which they are subdued, derives from their hardness of heart and can be removed if their heart is purified:

> You be hardened and you don't
> want to purify yourselves, to melt
> your feeling in the pure heart to
> obtain mercy by the great King.[41]

The exhortation of Hermas follows faithfully that of Jesus, why it is easier that the camel pass for the eye of a needle than a rich to give his own goods to the poor men (Mt 19,24).

From such framework the heads of the church, according to Hermas, are called to purify their heart to obtain mercy from God, with the purpose to desire the true life, that is the Truth and not the corruptible (material wealths) things, so as to be true educators on the earth: *"How can you educate the men chosen of God, if don't you be educated?"*.[42] For

---

[41] HERMAS, *Shepherd. Vision* 3,17,8-9. Ed. crit. F.X. FUNK-K. BIHLMEYER-M. WHITTAKER, *Die Apostolischen Väter. Griechisch-deutsche Parallelausgabe*, p. 360. Trad. di A. QUACQUARELLI, *I Padri Apostolici*, pp. 258-259.

[42] HERMAS, *Shepherd. Vision* 3,17,9,10. Ed. crit. F.X. FUNK-K. BIHLMEYER-M. WHITTAKER, *Die Apostolischen Väter.*

Hermas it's up to the heads of the church the obligation to purify their heart by the intemperance to live in peace, becoming concrete educators of the Truth.

Griechisch-deutsche Parallelausgabe, p. 360. Trad. di A. QUACQUARELLI, *I Padri Apostolici,* p. 259.

2. THE EDUCATIONAL MODEL FOR THE YOUNG PEOPLE

2.1. *The Educational Model of Christ*

Clement of Rome quotes the scriptural testimonium of Is 53,1 applying the appellative of little boy to Christ: " *He is as a little boy, as a root in the thirsty earth; he has neither appearance nor glory.*".[43] He shows to his community that, by the same standard as a little boy who is obedient to the orders of the Father since is subdued to his will, Christ has come in the world not in the boldness and in the pride, but in the humility:

> Christ is of the humble ones, not of the one who elevates himself on his flock. 2. The scepter of the majesty of God, the Lord Jesus Christ, didn't come in the din of the boldness and of the pride, - and he would have been able - but in the humility of heart as the Holy Spirit had to say of him.[44]

---

[43] CLEMENT of Rome, *Epistle to the Corinthians* 16,3. Ed. crit. F.X. FUNK-K. BIHLMEYER-M. WHITTAKER, *Die Apostolischen Väter. Griechisch-deutsche Parallelausgabe*, p. 96. Trad. di A. QUACQUARELLI, *I Padri Apostolici*, p. 59.

[44] CLEMENT of Rome, *Epistle to the Corinthians* 16,1-2. Ed. crit. F.X. FUNK-K. BIHLMEYER-M. WHITTAKER, *Die Apostolischen Väter. Griechisch-deutsche Parallelausgabe*, p. 96. Trad. di A. QUACQUARELLI, *I Padri Apostolici*, p. 59.

The image of the root, retaken from Isaiah, is meaningful in order to the humility of heart. With this image Clement wants to indicate that the humility of heart of Christ is comparable to the root, because the root is hidden in the earth, doesn't make itself see also supporting the earth. By the same standard as the root, Christ doesn't show and doesn't make to see his beautiful qualities, but he sustains the world, also showing no quality. He sustains the world since bears on himself the sins of the whole humanity and for this reason he hides the beauty of his face, appearing disfigured:

> We saw him, he didn't have a
> beautiful appearance, but his aspect
> was despicable, away from the
> aspect of the men.[45]

By the same standard as the root, Clement of Rome continues, also the afflicted man and without honour hides his face:

> As the man who is in the hits and in
> the suffering and who knows to bear
> the affliction because he hides his
> face, was not honoured and

---

[45] CLEMENT of Rome, *Epistle to the Corinthians* 16,3. Ed. crit. F.X. FUNK-K. BIHLMEYER-M. WHITTAKER, *Die Apostolischen Väter. Griechisch-deutsche Parallelausgabe*, p. 96. Trad. di A. QUACQUARELLI, *I Padri Apostolici*, p. 59.

calculated.[46]

Clement of Rome, referring to the image of the root that is without face since symbol of the humility, - by the same standard as a hit man, - places the virtue of the humility of heart to educational model for the community and for the same young people.
The educational model that Clement proposes to his community is founded on the humility, that is that particular predisposition of heart turned to bear the other people's lacks and to suffer for these, by the same standard as Christ who

> bears our sins and suffers for us, and
> we have considered that he was in
> the suffering, in the affliction and in
> the maltreatment.[47]

In the suffering and in the humility the man redeems himself, by the same standard as Jesus, because *"in the humiliation his condemnation was removed"*.[48] The sacrifices

---

[46] *Ibidem*

[47] CLEMENT of Rome, *Epistle to the Corinthians* 16,4. Ed. crit. F.X. FUNK-K. BIHLMEYER-M. WHITTAKER, *Die Apostolischen Väter. Griechisch-deutsche Parallelausgabe*, p. 96. Trad. di A. QUACQUARELLI, *I Padri Apostolici*, p. 59.

[48] CLEMENT of Rome, *Epistle to the Corinthians* 16,7. Ed. crit. F.X. FUNK-K. BIHLMEYER-M. WHITTAKER, *Die Apostolischen Väter. Griechisch-deutsche Parallelausgabe*, p. 98. Trad. di A. QUACQUARELLI, *I Padri Apostolici*, p. 60.

are intended by Clement of Rome as salutary remedies for the sinner soul, since because of these the Lord gives to this "*a long posterity*": "*If you make sacrifices for the sin, your soul will see a long posterity*".[49]

Clement of Rome exhorts the children to become participating in the education in Christ; education that a child can receive if he learns to be living torch of the same humility and of the same love that Christ has lived for us, powerful ramparts of true education and of salvation near God:

> Our children participate in the
> education in Christ; they learn what
> can the humility and the love near
> the Lord.[50]

Clement of Rome specifies that the educational model for the children has its base in the humility and in the love: from the union of both the virtues the child would participate in the same education of Christ; education that the Father has given to the Son from the very

---

[49] CLEMENT of Rome, *Epistole to the Corinthians* 16,11. Ed. crit. F.X. FUNK-K. BIHLMEYER-M. WHITTAKER, *Die Apostolischen Väter. Griechisch-deutsche Parallelausgabe*, p. 98. Trad. di A. QUACQUARELLI, *I Padri Apostolici*, p. 60.

[50] CLEMENT of Rome *Epistle to the Corinthians* 21,8. Ed. crit. F.X. FUNK-K. BIHLMEYER-M. WHITTAKER, *Die Apostolischen Väter. Griechisch-deutsche Parallelausgabe*, p. 106. Trad. di A. QUACQUARELLI, *I Padri Apostolici*, p. 64.

beginning of the creation and that he has made concrete in his highest form in the Easter Saturday (soteriological), where the Son in the humility of the cross has given himself for the salvation of the humanity.

It is not even excluded by the educational model of Christ the irreproachability, to which every young man can conform himself if he approaches himself the more possible to the purity and controls oneself in front of every form of evil:

> Equally the young people be irreproachable in everything, considering the purity and controlling oneself in front of every evil.[51]

According to Polycarp the conditions for becoming irreproachable men are the purity and the controlling oneself in front of every evil. Polycarp shows in the honesty the educational model of Christ for the young people, because the same Christ during his life maintained himself free by every form of material and moral contamination, since he was really him the healer of all the evils. To the eyes

---

[51] POLYCARP, *Letter to the Philippians* 5,3. Ed. crit. F.X. FUNK-K. BIHLMEYER-M. WHITTAKER, *Die Apostolischen Väter. Griechisch-deutsche Parallelausgabe*, p. 248. Trad. di A. QUACQUARELLI, *I Padri Apostolici*, p. 156.

of Christ, according to the pseudo-Clement, all the men are called children: *"As a father called us children and he saved us while we were for losing us"*.[52]

The pseudo-Clement, giving the appellative of father to Christ and connecting the salvation to the human progeny, wants make to understand to his community that Christ has loved the man, who was in the orgy of the corruptible goods, because he turned him to desire those eternal:

> blind of mind we adored stones, woods, gold, silver and bronze, works of men. All our life was death. We were surrounded by the darkness and full of so much obscurity in the eyes. For his will we regained the sight breaking the fog that envelopped us [53]

---

[52] Ps. CLEMENT, *Homily* 1,4. Ed. crit. F.X. FUNK-K. BIHLMEYER-M. WHITTAKER, *Die Apostolischen Väter. Griechisch-deutsche Parallelausgabe*, p. 154. Trad. di A. QUACQUARELLI, *I Padri Apostolici*, p. 221. For the concept of the conversion to the christianity as a educational process in the pseudo-clementines see P. GEMEINHARDT, *In Search of Christian Paideia Education and Conversion in Early Christian Biography* , in P. GEMEINHARDT, T. GEORGES, (Eds.), *Between Education and Conversion. Ways of Approaching Religion in Late Antiquity*, Berlin/Boston 2012 =*Zeitschrift für antikes Christentum* 16,1, pp. 88-98

[53] Ps. CLEMENT, *Homily* 1,6. Ed. crit. F.X. FUNK-K. BIHLMEYER-M. WHITTAKER, *Die Apostolischen Väter. Griechisch-deutsche Parallelausgabe*, p. 154. Trad. di A.

Because of the salvific love of Christ and of his great mercy, the man has been able to turn the look at the incorruptible goods: *"He had mercy of us and moved to pity he saved us"*.[54] Before the salvation and a good re-education to the eternal life there is the affliction, because every man suffers in reason of the gravity of his own actions: *"justly each one has suffered everything according to own actions.*[55]

Hermas specifies that those who operated badly are victims of different punishments and torments, which are re-poured on the man sinner on the base of his actions:

He (the angel of the punishment) takes those who have walked away from God walking in the way of the passions and of the pleasures of this world and he punish them, as each one has deserved, with different atrocious punishments.[56]

QUACQUARELLI, *I Padri Apostolici*, p. 221.

[54] Ps. CLEMENTE, *Homily* 1,7. Ed. crit. F.X. FUNK-K. BIHLMEYER-M. WHITTAKER, *Die Apostolischen Väter. Griechisch-deutsche Parallelausgabe*, p. 154. Trad. di A. QUACQUARELLI, *I Padri Apostolici*, pp. 303-304.

[55] HERMAS, *Shepherd. Similitudes* 63,6. Ed. crit. F.X. FUNK-K. BIHLMEYER-M. WHITTAKER, *Die Apostolischen Väter. Griechisch-deutsche Parallelausgabe*, pp. 454-456. Trad. di A. QUACQUARELLI, *I Padri Apostolici*, pp. 303-304.

[56] HERMAS, *Shepherd. Similitudes* 63,3-5. Ed. crit. F.X. FUNK-K.

From such framework the proofs of the life are due, according to Hermas, to the dissolute actions of those who have followed the pleasures and the passions:

the various experiences and punishments are the proofs of the life. Some people are punished with illnesses, others with deprivations, others with various illnesses, others with every misfortune; finally others are offended from unworthy and they suffer a lot of other evil. 5. Many uncertain in the decisions undertake a lot of things and nothing succeeds them. They say that don't have success in their business and, not by remembering in their heart that they operated badly, they blame the Lord. [57]

The affliction becomes a miraculous balm for the souls overwhelmed by the dissoluteness since, because of the tribulations through which the soul suffers the punishments inflicted by the angel of the punishment, the

BIHLMEYER-M. WHITTAKER, *Die Apostolischen Väter. Griechisch-deutsche Parallelausgabe*, p. 454. Trad. di A. QUACQUARELLI, *I Padri Apostolici*, p. 303.

[57] HERMAS, *Shepherd. Similitudes* 63,4-5. Ed. crit. F.X. FUNK-K. BIHLMEYER-M. WHITTAKER, *Die Apostolischen Väter. Griechisch-deutsche Parallelausgabe*, p. 454. Trad. di A. QUACQUARELLI, *I Padri Apostolici*, p. 303.

men, Hermas emphasizes,

> strengthen themselves in the faith
> of the Lord and, for the remaining
> days of their life, serve him with
> pure heart.[58]

The tribulations, according to Hermas, assume the connotation to be causes founding a good re-education, which gains ground after a profound contrition come from the awareness to have acted badly, whose concrete sign are the tribulations:

> When they are afflicted from every
> tribulation then they are delivered to
> me for a good re-education. They
> strengthen themselves in the faith of
> the Lord and, for the remaining
> days of their life, they serve him
> with pure heart. When they repent
> themselves then jump in their heart
> the perverse works that have
> made.[59]

The young people can reach such

---

[58] HERMAS, *Shepherd. Similitudes* 63,6. Ed. crit. F.X. FUNK-K. BIHLMEYER-M. WHITTAKER, *Die Apostolischen Väter. Griechisch-deutsche Parallelausgabe*, pp. 454-456. Trad. di A. QUACQUARELLI, *I Padri Apostolici*, p. 303.

[59] HERMAS, *Shepherd. Similitudes* 63,6. Ed. crit. F.X. FUNK-K. BIHLMEYER-M. WHITTAKER, *Die Apostolischen Väter. Griechisch-deutsche Parallelausgabe*, pp. 454-456. Trad. di A. QUACQUARELLI, *I Padri Apostolici*, pp. 303-304.

destination, Polycarp explains, if they flee the passions of the world, since the flesh makes war on the spirit:

It is beautiful to be detached from the passions of the world, because every passion makes war on the spirit, and neither the fornicators, nor the effeminate and the sodomites men will inherit the kingdom of God, not even those who make strangeness. For this it needs that they be far from all these evils and subdued to the presbyteries and to the deacons as to God and to Christ.[60]

It resounds the pauline thought of the fight of the flesh against the spirit and vice versa (Gal 5,17). In fact according to the apostle Paul those who follow the pleasures of the world are not pleasing to God because don't behave as he instead would want and, consequently, don't inherit the kingdom of God, (1Cor 6,9-10). One perceive by intuition that the young ones are called to do own the educational model of Christ, based on the apathy, that is to say on the escape from all the passions that the world has if they let

---

[60] POLYCARP, *Letter to the Philippians* 5,3. Ed. crit. F.X. FUNK-K. BIHLMEYER-M. WHITTAKER, *Die Apostolischen Väter. Griechisch-deutsche Parallelausgabe,* p. 248. Trad. di A. QUACQUARELLI, *I Padri Apostolici,* p. 156.

themselves infatuate.

2.2. *The Educational Model of the True Christian Sage*

2.2.1. Faithful And Wise Men

The fidelity and the wisdom are two virtues (habits) of the soul of the faithful and sage men, virtues that, according to Clement of Rome, are at the base of a life lived according to a good education that concretely appears since their youth with correct ways: "*We have sent to you faithful and wise men, lived in the middle of us with correct ways by the youth to the old age*".[61] The sending on behalf of Clement of Rome men's well educated has been depended by the possession, on behalf of them, of these two virtues, of the fidelity and of the wisdom; virtues that have produced in them correct attitudes, having been living copies of the fidelity and of the wisdom of the

---

[61] CLEMENT of Rome, *Epistle to the Corinthians* 63,3. Ed. crit. F.X. FUNK-K. BIHLMEYER-M. WHITTAKER, *Die Apostolischen Väter. Griechisch-deutsche Parallelausgabe*, p. 148. Trad. di A. QUACQUARELLI, *I Padri Apostolici*, p. 92.

Logos who, in the primordial Saturday, was faithful to the Father and he turned to him because eternal wisdom of the Father.

The fidelity and the wisdom are marked by Clement as exemplaries virtues because those who have been educated according to these, are living witnesses of the incarnate Truth: *"that they will be witnesses between we and you"*.[62]

2.2.2. Germanic, Model of Youth

In the *Polycarp's martyrdom* Germanic is marked as a model of youth because educated to the values of the Christian *paideia*; *paideia* that manifests in Germanic his own power of sustain towards the weak ones and of victory against the strengths of the evil through these three virtues: the generosity, the constancy and the highness of the soul. The first two are at the base of his sustain for the Christians who, for their weakness, bore atrocious torments to enjoy already on the earth the eternal life:

Taken by the grace of Christ, they

---

[62] *Ibidem*

despised the torments of the world, acquiring themselves, for a single moment, the eternal life (.). Likewise those who were convicted to the wild animals bore horrible torments, stretched out on shells and tortured with other forms of various tortures, because it is sought, if it had been possible, to induce them to the abnegation. 3,1 (.). The generous Germanic with his constancy sustained their weakness and he was admirable in the struggle against the wild animals.[63]

The generosity, united to the constancy, is not only at the base of the sustain of the spirit of those Christians who suffered atrocious torments because of their faith and following the incarnate (Christ) truth, but also of their victory against the wild animals, tenses to satisfy only the needs of the flesh. In the *Polycarp's martyrdom* Germanic is marked as the youthful model of the education, that is to say of the one who undertakes, both with the word and with the actions, because the other ones become strong in the spirit, winning in the

---

[63] *Polycarp's martyrdom* 2,3-4.3,1. Ed. crit. F.X. FUNK-K. BIHLMEYER-M. WHITTAKER, *Die Apostolischen Väter.Griechisch-deutsche Parallelausgabe*, pp. 262-264. Trad. di A. QUACQUARELLI, *I Padri Apostolici*, p. 162.

struggle against the tendencies of the flesh, included the wild animals. With his generosity and his constancy Germanic educates the Christians, tormented by the atrocity of the tortures, to sustain the weakness of their body because the suffering of their body induces the spirit to become stronger for being guide of the body, or better its coachman.

It recurs the thought of the anonymous author according to whom the soul reinvigorates itself and sustains the body when she succeeds in taking the reins of its government,[64] or when the body is in prey to the suffering. Germanic is also a formidable example of victorious educator against the tendencies of the flesh, ever since the flesh fights the spirit and makes war on it, referring to the words of the anonymous author of the *To Diognetus*, because this wants to turn it towards the things of the earth: "*The soul loves the flesh that hates her, and the members: so also the Christians love those who hate them*".[65] In the eyes of the crowd Germanic becomes example

---

[64] *To Diognetus* 5,5. Ed. crit. F.X. FUNK-K. BIHLMEYER-M. WHITTAKER, *Die Apostolischen Väter. Griechisch-deutsche Parallelausgabe*, p. 312. Trad. di E. NORELLI, *A Diogneto*, p. 89.

[65] *To Diognetus* 6,6. Ed. crit. F.X. FUNK-K. BIHLMEYER-M. WHITTAKER, *Die Apostolischen Väter. Griechisch-deutsche Parallelausgabe*, pp. 312-314. Trad. di E. NORELLI, *A Diogneto*, p. 96.

of highness of the soul ever since he provoked the wild animals to eat him alive:

The proconsul while exhorted him saying to have pity of his youth, he inciting him attracted against himself the beast, desirous to escape as soon as possible from this unfair and iniquitous life. 2. Therefore all the crowd marveled of the highness of the soul of the pious and generous race of the Christians.[66]

From such framework Germanic becomes model of true educator of the Spirit, because, by one side, sustaining the weakness of the flesh of the Christians, he shares their suffering that is salutary for the spirit since this doesn't remain wrapped by the unbridled orgies of this, and because, by the other, he wins on the unjust and iniquitous desires of the flesh, freeing the spirit by the jail of this, in the giving oneself and in the giving the body of the Christians to the wild animals to be eaten.

---

[66] *Polycarp's, martyrdom* 3,1-2. Ed. crit. F.X. FUNK-K. BIHLMEYER-M. WHITTAKER, *Die Apostolischen Väter. Griechisch-deutsche Parallelausgabe*, p. 264. Trad. di A. QUACQUARELLI, *I Padri Apostolici*, pp. 162-163.

CONCLUSION

In this study we have had the opportunity to see that, according to the apostolic Fathers, what allows the educational practice of the parents is not only the presence of one who is to be educated, but above all the firm predisposition of the educators to draw near to the Truth both with the mind and the actions. According to the apostolic Fathers this progressive walk, on behalf of the educators, plays a fundamental role for their educational practice, because the educators, removing all the lowest tendencies of the flesh, can transmit to the young ones their education founded on the virtues, education that had not only been transmitted by the same Christ, on the trail of whom the young ones have the duty to imitate his behavior, but also by the wise and faithful men and by the men of faith who, as Germanic, have given example of victory, fortifying the Spirit, on the weaknesses of the flesh.

ESSENTIAL BIBLIOGRAPHY

FUNK F.X. - BIHLMEYER WHITTAKER M., *Die Apostolischen Väter. Griechisch - deutsche Parallelausgabe*, Tubingen 1992.

GEMEINHARDT, P., *In Search of Christian Paideia Education and Conversion in Early Christian Biography* , in P. GEMEINHARDT, T. GEORGES, (Eds.), *Between Education and Conversion. Ways of Approaching Religion in Late Antiquity*, Berlin/Boston 2012 =*Zeitschrift für antikes Christentum* 16,1, pp. 88-98.

LEYERLE B., *Children and 'the Child' in Early Christianity*, in J.E. GRUBBS-T. PARKIN (Eds.), *The Oxford Handbook of Childhood and education in the classical world*, Oxford University

Press 2013, pp. 559-579.

MARROU H.I., *Histoire de l'éducation dans l'antiquité*, Éditions du Seuil 1965.

MITCHELL M.M.-F.M. YOUNG, *The Cambridge History of Christianity*, vol. 1, *Origins to Constantine*, Cambridge University Press 2008, pp. 82-487.

QUACQUARELLI A., *I Padri apostolici*, Rome 2000.

STRAWBRIDGE J., '*A School of Paul? Pauline Texts in Early Christian Schooltext Papyri,*' in M. HAUGE – A. PITTS (Eds.) *Ancient Education and Early* Christianity (LNTS; New York: T&T Clark 2016.

Finito di stampare nel mese di Ottobre 2017
per conto di Youcanprint *Self-Publishing*